The Tax Cuts and Jobs Act of 2017
Tax Windfall or Tax Disaster???

Eight Major Changes of the New Tax Law

How the New Tax Law will Affect Your Family and Your Business

Larry M. Weinstein, CPA
The Tax Terminator®

This book presents information that is factual as of the time of publication. The information presented here is of a general nature.

How the IRS rules and regulations should best be applied is different in every taxpayer's unique case. Accordingly, no liability can be assumed in how the information is applied to your particular personal situation.

No client relationship has been
created or can be inferred by purchase of this book.

Table of Contents

Introduction

The Tax Cuts and Jobs Act of 2017 was passed by Congress and signed into law on December 22, 2017, and is the most significant change to the tax law in over 30 years.

Many changes were made that affect both individuals and businesses and their owners.

Hopefully, many smart taxpayers and their tax advisors, will learn about these changes, how it affects them and their businesses and more importantly, how to use these changes to LEGALLY lower your tax bill.

This guide is meant to give you an overview of the new Tax Law, organized into 8 main topic areas.

These topics are meant to highlight the changes most likely to have the most significant impact on business owners.

These topics are meant to provide an overview of the most important changes of the tax code that you need to understand today.

The final language of the final bill was 1,097 pages. It is impossible to give a comprehensive analysis of all the changes big and small, in this report.

Some parts of the new law seem incomplete and ambiguous and it will likely take years before regulations and court rulings provide definitive guidance to all of the changes.

You cannot assume that any previous tax planning done is still appropriate based upon the new laws. As a business owner, you CANNOT wait until 2019 to begin strategic tax planning... only to discover you missed opportunities to lower your taxes significantly by not planning in 2018.

If you need assistance in working through and understanding these new changes and how they affect you and your business, I look forward to hearing from you.

I wish you all the best in using these changes in the tax law to LEGALLY reduce your taxes!!

Larry M. Weinstein, CPA
Certified Tax Resolution Specialist®
Houston, Texas

ONE

Changes to Individual Income Tax Brackets

The new tax laws lowered the tax rates from a maximum rate of 39.6% to 37%.

Additionally, the tax brackets were "widened" to allow more income to be taxed at the lower tax rates.

The effect of these changes in both the tax rates and the tax brackets will likely result in lower taxes for individuals.

Income Tax Rates for Single Taxpayers			
2018		2017	
10%	$0-$9,525	10%	$0-$9,325
12%	$9,526-$38,700	15%	$9,326-$37,950
22%	$38,701-$82,500	25%	$37,951-$91,900
24%	$82,501-$157,500	28%	$91,901-$191,650
32%	$157,501-$200,000	33%	$191,651-$416,700
35%	$200,001-$500,000	35%	$416,701-$418,400
37%	$500,001 or more	39.6%	$418,401 or more

Income Tax Rates for Married Filing Jointly Taxpayers			
2018		2017	
10%	$0-$19,050	10%	$0-$18,650
12%	$19,051-$77,400	15%	$18,651-$75,900
22%	$77,401-$165,000	25%	$75,901-$153,100
24%	$165,001-$315,000	28%	$153,101-$233,350
32%	$315,001-$400,000	33%	$233,351-$416,700
35%	$400,001-$600,000	35%	$416,701-$470,700
37%	$600,001 or more	39.6%	$470,701 or more

TWO

Standard Deductions Increase Means Fewer Itemized Deductions

One of the stated goals of this round of tax reform was simplification for the individual taxpayer. Whether this happens remains to be seen!!

Based upon the premise of simplification, the Standard Deduction was increased to offset the limitations on various elements of itemized deductions. See below.

Filing Status	2017	2018
Single	$6,350	$12,000
Married Filing Jointly	$12,700	$24,000
Married Filing Separately	$6,350	$12,000
Head of Household	$9,350	$18,000

It is still more advantageous for some taxpayers to itemize, however, limits have been placed on many items that have been fully deductible in prior years.

Mortgage Interest

Mortgages that closed after 12/15/17 (or 4/1/18 if a written contract existed prior to year-end 12/31/2017) have a mortgage limitation on mortgages greater than $750,000. Existing mortgages remain unchanged. For existing mortgages, there is a limitation of deductibility of interest for mortgages greater than $1 million. ***Negative impact for taxpayers with larger home/ mortgages.***

Home Equity Loan Interest

Beginning in 2018, interest on Home Equity Lines of Credit (HELOC) is no longer deductible.

State and Local Taxes (SALT)

Deduction for state and local income taxes is now limited to $10,000 annually for most filing statuses. (Married filing separately is limited to $5,000 annually). ***Negative impact to taxpayers with larger, more expensive homes and taxpayers who live in areas with high state and local tax rates.***

Miscellaneous Itemized Deductions

Deductions limited to 2% of Adjusted Gross Income have been completely eliminated. Examples include investment advisory fees, un-reimbursed business expenses, tax preparation fees and certain attorney fees. ***Negative impact to taxpayers who incur these type of expenses.***

Charitable Contributions

Charitable contributions are still deductible, however, you will only receive a tax benefit if you are able to itemize (Itemized deductions are greater than standard deduction). ***Tax Tip: If you are near the itemized deduction/standard deduction threshold for deductibility, it may make sense to "bunch" your charitable contributions into a single tax year to secure the deduction.***

Moving Expenses

Moving expenses are no longer tax deductible, unless the taxpayer is a member of the Armed Forces and the move is due to a permanent station change.

Casualty and Theft Losses

Beginning in 2018, there is **NO deductio**n for a casualty or theft **UNLESS** the loss takes place in a Federally Declared Disaster Area. ***Tax Tip: Consider reviewing your insurance policies including flood insurance to insure you are adequately covered given the loss of tax deductibility.***

The Good News for high income taxpayers who still choose to itemize is the elimination of the phaseout of itemized deductions based upon income.

THREE

Elimination of Personal Exemptions

Prior to 2018, taxpayers were entitled to a tax deduction of a personal exemption of $4,050 per person claimed on the tax return, (subject to phaseouts, based upon income).

Effective 1/1/2018, all personal exemptions have been completely eliminated. It is intended that the elimination of personal exemptions will be offset by the increase in the Standard Deduction. See Section 2 above.

Negative impact to taxpayers with more children/ personal exemptions (more than 4 personal exemptions) and especially families with dependent children older than age 17, for example college students and families that are caring for elderly parents for which you are providing more than 50% of their support.

FOUR

Other Changes That Affect Taxable Personal Income

Child Tax Credit

The Child Tax Credit has been increased to $2,000 per qualifying child (previously $1,000). The phaseout limits have also been increased to $400,000 for Married Filing Jointly and $200,000 for Single Filers.

A $500 credit is allowed for any dependent not a qualifying child.

The refundable portion of the Child Tax Credit (refund greater than tax liability) is limited to $1,400.

Child Tax Rates

The "Kiddie Tax" has been eliminated. A child's tax will be calculated according to their own tax rate, based upon their income level.

Previously, a dependent child's investment income was taxed at the usually higher rate of their parent.

Alternative Minimum Tax

The long dreaded Alternative Tax (AMT) has higher exemption

amounts. While not gone completely, it is expected to impact fewer individuals. This is good news as the AMT has been consistently capturing more and more individuals that had no significant "tax preference" items.

529 Savings Plans

Beginning in 2018, $10,000 per student can now be used for elementary through high school tuition.

Use of 529 funds are not subject to the $10,000 per year annual limitation.

Gift Taxes

The Gift Tax exclusion had a modest increase to $15,000 per person per year from $14,000.

Estate Taxes

The exemption for estate taxes has slightly more than doubled, to $11,200,00 for individuals (from $5,490,000) and $22,400,00 for married couples (from $10,980,000).

This is good news individuals with estates between $5,4900,000 and $11,200,000 and for married couples with estates between $10,980,000 and $22,400,000.

High net worth individuals may consider revisiting their estate and gifting strategy, given the recent changes to the gift and estate tax law!!

FIVE

Changes for 2019 and Beyond

Affordable Care Act

You will no longer be subject to a penalty if you do not purchase individual health insurance; The "Individual Mandate" under the Affordable Care Act goes away. The "Shared Responsibility" payment owed by a taxpayer for NOT enrolling in a health insurance plan is repealed beginning in 2019.

Divorcing and Divorced Taxpayers

Alimony payments will no longer be deductible by the payor, nor will alimony be includible and taxable in income for divorce agreements and divorce settlements beginning in 2019 and later.

All agreements and settlements entered into before 2019 are considered "grandfathered in" (they are still deductible by the payor and taxable to the recipient).

> *Note: Some of these changes are temporary.*
> *Many of the individual tax rate changes are scheduled to revert back to the old code after 2025.*

SIX

Tax Changes for Business Owners & Professional Practices

The Biggest Tax Cut in 30 Years—Qualified Business Income (QBI)

The biggest change in the new Tax Law is clearly reflected in the 20% Exclusion of Qualified Business Income (QBI).

The new QBI deduction is very complicated even though Congress intended for it to be simple.

The major points of confusion is the way in which different types of businesses can be treated differently for the QBI deduction phase out.

Pass-through income from S Corporations, sole proprietorships, partnerships and LLCs that are "qualified trade or business" can possibly receive up to a 20% deduction of their income generated from the qualified trade or business.

Income from real estate assets would typically fall under QBI tax treatment.

The result of a QBI deduction is a lower income tax rate on the pass-through business income.

Exceptions

Wages you are paid as an S Corporation shareholder do not count as qualifying business income, and therefore, don't receive the 20% deduction.

This does not mean that S Corporations are no longer advantageous compared to other pass-through options. The IRS still requires S corporation shareholders to take a reasonable salary.

There are certain exclusions for qualified businesses where generally the income is produced from the skill and or reputation of an individual.

QBI Deduction Limitation for a "Specified Service Businesses"

For businesses that are defined as "specified service businesses", the QBI deduction is phased out for taxable income between $315,000 and $415,000 for married filing jointly taxpayers and $157,000 to $207,500 for individuals and heads of household.

QBI Deduction Limitations for Non-"Specified Service Businesses"

For taxpayers with personal taxable income greater than $315,000 (married filing jointly) or $157,500 (single), the 20% QBI Deduction may be limited.

The QBI Deduction phases out between $315,000 and $415,000 (married filing jointly) and $157,500 and $207,500 (single).

For individuals and businesses subject to this phaseout, the 20% QBI Deduction **MAY** be limited to the greater of:

1) 50% of **ALL** W-3 wages paid for the business (using the owners pro-rata share) or

2) the sum of 25% of **ALL** W-3 wages **PLUS** 2.5% of the unadjusted cost basis of all qualified business property (using the owners pro-rata share).

SEVEN

Are C Corporations About to Make a Comeback?

The tax rates have changed for C Corporations.

C Corporations file and pay their own taxes. C Corporation income is now taxed a flat 21%.

The tax rates pre-2018 were graduated and ranged from a low of 15% to a high of 34%.

Personal service corporation's were taxed at a flat 35%. In the past, C Corporations were taxed at a higher rate and did not always make much sense to use.

It may now be worth looking more closely at C Corporations now versus other options.Income from real estate assets would typically fall under QBI tax treatment.

Please note that C Corporations are NOT a pass-through entity and accordingly, are NOT subject to the new rules for Qualified Business Income.

EIGHT

Other Various Changes Affecting Business Taxes

Accrual Method of Accounting

In the new tax law starting in 2018, all entities including C Corporations and all of the flow-through entities, are allowed to use the cash basis method of accounting for tax purposes if their average gross receipts for the past three years or less than $25 million.

Depreciation

No longer are computers considered listed property. This will make them easier to depreciate more quickly.

Section 179 Depreciation

The annual section 179 depreciation limit has been increased from $510,000 up to $1 million.

The threshold for section 179 phaseout was increased to $2.5 million.

Bonus depreciation (100%) is now allowed on both USED and new equipment.

The net effect of all of these changes to depreciation means it will be easier to expense business assets in the first year.

Business Interest Deductions

The deduction for business interest is now limited to 30% of earnings before interest, taxes, depreciation and amortization (EBITDA).

This limitation does not apply to motor vehicles using floor plans.

Net Operating Losses (NOLs)

Net operating losses from a business can no longer be carried back. They can only be carried forward. The carry-forward can only be used to offset 80% of taxable income.

Like Kind Exchanges (Section 1031)

Section 1031 like kind exchanges are now only allowed for real estate.

Fringe Benefits/Entertainment Expenses

Items such as office food for employees are not subject to a 50% meals and entertainment deduction limitation.

The deduction for entertainment expenses has been completely eliminated!

Uniform Capitalization Rules (UNICAP)

The Uniform Capitalization Rules for calculating inventory will now only apply if the three-year gross receipts average is greater than $25 million.

Now It's Up to You to Take the Next Step!!

Even under normal circumstances, doing Strategic Tax Planning to LEGALLY minimizing your taxes is difficult, and is partially art and partially science.

The newly passed Tax Law, while being beneficial to many taxpayers, is complex, and hard-to-understand even for the professionals.

It is now more important than ever, to work with a trusted CPA Tax Advisor, who understands you and your business and how to best utilize the new and continually changing tax laws to LEGALLY maximize your tax savings.

You cannot assume that any previous tax planning done is still appropriate based upon the new laws. As a business owner, you CANNOT wait until 2019 to begin strategic tax planning... only to discover you missed opportunities to lower your taxes significantly by not planning in 2018.

If you need assistance in working through and understanding these new changes and how they affect you and your business, I look forward to hearing from you.

Made in the USA
Monee, IL
04 November 2026

67384916R00015